Inventory and Purchasing
Exam Prep Guide

PEARSON
Prentice Hall

Upper Saddle River, New Jersey
Columbus, Ohio

NATIONAL RESTAURANT ASSOCIATION SOLUTIONS™

DISCLAIMER:

The information presented in this publication is provided for informational purposes only and is not intended to provide legal advice or establish standards of reasonable behavior. Customers who develop food safety-related or operational policies and procedures are urged to obtain the advice and guidance of legal counsel. Although **National Restaurant Association Solutions, LLC (NRA Solutions)** endeavors to include accurate and current information compiled from sources believed to be reliable, **NRA Solutions**, and its **licensor, the National Restaurant Association Educational Foundation (NRAEF)**, distributors, and agents make no representations or warranties as to the accuracy, currency, or completeness of the information. No responsibility is assumed or implied by the NRAEF, NRA Solutions, distributors, or agents for any damage or loss resulting from inaccuracies or omissions or any actions taken or not taken based on the content of this publication.

Sample questions are designed to familiarize the student with format, length and style of the examination questions, and represent only a sampling of topic coverage. The performance level on sample questions does not guarantee passing of a ManageFirst Program examination. Further, the distribution of sample exam questions with their focus on particular areas of subject matter within a ManageFirst Competency Guide is not necessarily reflective of how the questions will be distributed across subject matter on the actual correlating ManageFirst exam.

Visit www.restaurant.org for information on other National Restaurant Association Solutions products and programs.

ManageFirst Program™, ServSafe®, and ServSafe Alcohol® are registered trademarks or trademarks of the National Restaurant Association Educational Foundation, used under license by National Restaurant Association Solutions, LLC a wholly owned subsidiary of the National Restaurant Association.

Copyright © 2009 National Restaurant Association Educational Foundation. Published by Pearson Education, Inc., Upper Saddle River, New Jersey 07458. All rights reserved. Printed in the United States of America. No part of this document may be reproduced, stored in a retrieval system, or transmitted in any form or by any other means electronic, mechanical, photocopying, recording, scanning or otherwise, except as permitted under Section 107 and 108 of the 1976 United States Copyright Act, without prior written permission of the publisher.

Requests for permission to use or reproduce material from this book should be directed to:
Copyright Permissions
National Restaurant Association Solutions
175 West Jackson Boulevard, Suite 1500
Chicago, IL 60604
Phone: 312-715-1010   Fax: 312-566-9729
Email: permissions@restaurant.org

10 9 8 7 6 5 4 3 2 1
ISBN-13: 978-0-13-812690-2
ISBN-10:   0-13-812690-9

Contents

How to Take the ManageFirst Examination	1
Chapter Summaries and Objectives	9
Inventory and Purchasing Practice Questions	15
Answer Key	25
Explanations to Answers	27
Glossary	39

How to Take the ManageFirst Examination

The ability to take tests effectively is a learned skill. There are specific things you can do to prepare yourself physically and mentally for an exam. This section helps you prepare and do your best on the ManageFirst Examination.

I. BEFORE THE EXAM

A. *How to Study*
Study the right material the right way. There is a lot of information and material in each course. How do you know what to study so you are prepared for the exam? This guide highlights what you need to know.

1. **Read the Introduction to each *Competency Guide*.** The beginning section of each guide explains the features and how it is organized.

2. **Look at how each chapter is organized and take clues from the book.**

   - *The text itself is important.* If the text is bold, large, or italicized you can be sure it is a key point that you should understand.

   - *The very first page tells you what you will learn.*

     Inside This Chapter: This tells you at a high level what will be covered in the chapter. Make sure you understand what each section covers. If you have studied the chapter but cannot explain what each section pertains to, you need to review that material.

Learning Objectives: After completing each chapter, you should be able to accomplish the specific goals and demonstrate what you have learned after reading the material. The practice exam as well as the actual exam questions relate to these learning objectives.

- *Quizzes and Tests*

    Test Your Knowledge: This is a pretest found at the beginning of each chapter to see how much you already know. Take this quiz to help you determine which areas you need to study and focus on.

- *Key Terms* are listed at the beginning of each chapter and set in bold the first time they are referred to in the chapter. These terms—new and specific to the topic or ones you are already familiar with—are key to understanding the chapter's content. When reviewing the material, look for the key terms you don't know or understand and review the corresponding paragraph.

- *Exhibits* visually depict key concepts and include charts, tables, photographs, and illustrations. As you review each chapter, find out how well you can explain the concepts illustrated in the exhibits.

- *Additional Exercises*

    Think About It sidebars are designed to provoke further thought and/or discussion and require understanding of the topics.

    Activity boxes are designed to check your understanding of the material and help you apply your knowledge. The activities relate to a learning objective.

- *Summary* reviews all the important concepts in the chapter and helps you retain and master the material.

3. **Attend Review Sessions or Study Groups**. Review sessions, if offered, cover material that will most likely be on the test. If separate review sessions are not offered, make sure you attend class the day before the exam. Usually, the instructor will review the material during this class. If you are a social learner, study with other students; discussing the topics with other students may help your comprehension and retention.

4. **Review the Practice Questions,** which are designed to help you prepare for the exam. Sample questions are designed to familiarize the student with the format, length, and style of the exam questions, and represent only a sampling of topic coverage on the final exam. The performance level on sample questions does not guarantee passing of a ManageFirst Program exam.

B. *How to Prepare Physically and Mentally*

Make sure you are ready to perform your best during the exam. Many students do everything wrong when preparing for an exam. They stay up all night, drink coffee to stay awake, or take sleep aids which leave them groggy and tired on test day.

There are practical things to do to be at your best. If you were an athlete preparing for a major event, what would you do to prepare yourself? You wouldn't want to compete after staying up all night or drinking lots of caffeine. The same holds true when competing with your brain!

1. **Get plenty of sleep.** Lack of sleep makes it difficult to focus and recall information. Some tips to help you get a good night's sleep are:

    - Make sure you have studied adequately enough days before the exam so that you do not need to cram and stay up late the night before the test.
    - Eat a good dinner the night before and a good breakfast the day of the exam.
    - Do not drink alcohol or highly-caffeinated drinks.
    - Exercise during the day, but not within four hours of bedtime.
    - Avoid taking sleep aids.

2. **Identify and control anxiety.** It is important to know the difference between actual test anxiety and anxiety caused by not being prepared.

Test anxiety is an actual physical reaction. If you know the information when you are **not** under pressure but feel physically sick and cannot recall information during the exam, you probably suffer from test anxiety. In this case, you may need to learn relaxation techniques or get some counseling. The key is how you react under pressure.

If you cannot recall information during reviews or the practice exam when you are not under pressure, you have not committed the information to memory and need to study more.

- Make sure you are as prepared as possible. (See "Anxiety Caused by Lack of Preparation")
- Take the exam with a positive attitude.
- Do not talk to other students who may be pessimistic or negative about the exam.
- Know what helps you relax and do it (chewing gum, doodling, breathing exercises).
- Make sure you understand the directions. Ask the instructor questions *before* the test begins.
- The instructor or proctor may only talk to you if you have defective materials or need to go to the restroom. They cannot discuss any questions.
- The instructor or proctor may continuously monitor the students so do not be nervous if they walk around the room.
- Know the skills described in Section II, During the Test.

3. **Anxiety Caused by Lack of Preparation.** The best way to control anxiety due to lack of preparation is focus on the exam. Whenever possible, you should know and do the following:

- Know the location of the exam and how to get there.
- Know if it is a paper-and-pencil test or an online exam. Pencils may be available but bring sufficient number 2 pencils if taking the paper-and-pencil version of the exam.
- If it is an online exam you may need your email address, if you have one, to receive results.
- You are prohibited from using purses, books, papers, pagers, cell phones, or other recording devices during the exam.
- Calculators and scratch paper may be used, if needed. Be sure your calculator is working properly and has fresh batteries.
- The exam is not a timed; however, it is usually completed in less than two hours.
- Take the sample exam so you know what format, style, and content to expect.
- Arrive early so you don't use valuable testing time to unpack.

II. DURING THE TEST

An intent of National Restaurant Association Solutions' ManageFirst exams is to make sure you have met certain learning objectives. If you are physically prepared, have studied the material, and taken the practice exam, you should find the ManageFirst exams to be very valid and fair. Remember, successful test taking is a skill. Understanding the different aspects of test preparation and exam taking will help ensure your best performance.

A. *Test Taking Strategies*

- Preview the exam for a quick overview of the length and questions.
- Do not leave any question unanswered.
- Answer the questions you are sure of first.

- Stop and check occasionally to make sure you are putting your answer in the correct place on the answer sheet. If you are taking an online exam, you will view one question at a time.
- Do not spend too much time on any one question. If you do not know the answer after reasonable consideration, move on and come back to it later.
- Make note of answers about which you are unsure so you can return to them.
- Review the exam at the end to check your answers and make sure all questions are answered.

B. Strategies for Answering Multiple-Choice Questions

Multiple-choice tests are objective. The correct answer is there, you just need to identify it.

- Try to answer the question before you look at the options.
- Use the process of elimination. Eliminate the answers you know are incorrect.
- Your first response is usually correct.

III. AFTER THE EXAM

Learn from each exam experience so you can do better on the next. If you did not perform on the exam as you expected, determine the reason. Was it due to lack of studying or preparation? Were you unable to control your test anxiety? Were you not focused enough because you were too tired? Identifying the reason allows you to spend more time on that aspect before your next exam. Use the information to improve on your next exam.

If you do not know the reason, you should schedule a meeting with the instructor. As all NRA Solutions ManageFirst exams are consistent, it is important to understand and improve your exam performance. If you cannot identify your problem areas, your errors will most likely be repeated on consecutive exams.

IV. EXAM DAY DETAILS

The information contained in this section will help ensure that you are able to take the exam on the scheduled test day and that you know what to expect and are comfortable about taking the exam.

- Have your photo identification available.
- Anyone with special needs must turn in an *Accommodation Request* to the instructor at least 10 days prior to the exam to receive approval and allow time for preparations. *If needs are not known 10 days prior, you may not be able to take the exam on the scheduled test day.*
- A bilingual English-native language dictionary may be used by anyone who speaks English as a second language. The dictionary will be inspected to make sure there are no notes or extra papers in it.
- If you are ill and must leave the room after the exam has begun you must turn in your materials to the instructor or proctor. If you are able to return, your materials will be returned to you and you may complete the exam. If it is an online exam you must close your browser and if the exam has not been graded yet, login in again when you return.
- Restroom breaks are allowed. Only one person may go at a time and all materials must be turned in prior to leaving the room and picked up when you return; or you must close your browser and login again for online exams.
- Make-up tests may be available if you are unable to take the exam on test day. Check with your instructor for details.
- If you are caught cheating you will not receive a score and must leave the exam location.

Inventory and Purchasing Chapter Summaries and Objectives

Chapter 1 Introduction to Inventory and Purchasing

Summary

The purchasing function occupies an important role within the restaurant or foodservice industry and greatly contributes to a restaurant or foodservice operation's bottom line. A purchaser must ensure than an adequate supply of product is available for sale to customers, the product is consistently of the desired quality, the operation is investing a minimal amount of its available cash, and the product is obtained at or below the price that competitors are paying.

Failing to meet these objectives can damage the operation's reputation, limit the business' ability to meet its future financial obligations, reduce an operation's profitability, and put it at a competitive disadvantage.

A restaurant or foodservice operation must purchase a wide variety of goods ad services in order to operate. Examples include food, beverages, equipment, and services, some of which can be purchased or leased.

After completing this chapter, you should be able to:
- Define purchasing, procurement, and product selection.
- Outline the objectives in the purchasing function.
- Describe the importance of maintaining an operation's competitive position.
- List the types of goods and services that might be purchased by a foodservice organization.

Chapter 2 The Purchasing Function

Summary

Whether buying is performed by an owner/manager or organized into a larger buying department, the actions and decisions related to purchasing impact all of the operation's employees, from managers to hourly staff. Part of your responsibilities as a purchaser is to ensure that you provide the right goods and services to the operation's employees in a manner approved by your supervisor. Failure to do this can lead to inefficient work processes, budget difficulties, and employee and customer dissatisfaction.

A person performing the purchasing function must possess qualities that categorically can be placed in four purchasing skill sets: technical, conceptual, interpersonal, and other qualities. A purchaser's job description will be shaped by the specific operation's policies and needs, and should include duties that relate to these skill sets.

The rules and guidelines concerning ethics in purchasing are there to protect all the parties involved. Most operations have a written code of ethics that purchasers must commit to following. Kickbacks, accepting gifts, reciprocity, free samples, and personal purchases are all areas of ethical concern.

While it is important for you to know how to handle these ethical challenges, most of your time as a purchaser will be spent dealing with the many day-to-day administrative activities of the job, which can be overwhelming if not managed appropriately. There are also some common challenges related to purchasing that you must know how to address quickly in order to ensure the purchasing function runs smoothly in your operation. These range from vendor management to receiving and storing maintenance to effective time management.

After completing this chapter, you should be able to:
- Describe how the purchasing function is organized in a foodservice operation.
- Summarize the knowledge, skills, and abilities a purchaser must possess.
- Describe the duties and responsibilities of purchasers.
- Describe ethical considerations related to purchasing.
- Identify issues involved in administering purchasing activities.

Chapter 3 Quality Standards in Purchasing

Summary

Quality standards describe the measures of excellence a foodservice operation seeks to satisfy. They not only reflect an operation's locale and clientele, but they also serve as cost controls and tools that can be used to uphold alignment between purchasers and suppliers. Quality standards pronounce quality expectations to customers. They serve as parameters for suppliers who submit bid proposals and list every important consideration of the operation's food and nonfood products and services.

Many factors and influences affect quality standards and must be considered prior to writing the operation's product specifications. To assist them, purchasers may choose to perform a make-or-buy analysis to determine the best possible relationship between a product's desired quality and edible portion cost.

Many people may offer input into what an operation's quality standards should be. However, it is the responsibility of the owner and/or purchaser to ensure that all internal and external stakeholders know and adhere to them.

After completing this chapter, you should be able to:
- Identify and communicate quality standards.
- Identify factors contributing to the establishment of quality standards.

- State why it is important to convey and adhere to quality standards.
- Describe buyer considerations when conducting a make-or-buy analysis.

Chapter 4 The Procurement Process and Supplier Selection

Summary

While there are many considerations in the procurement and supplier selection process, an operation's mission, goals, and quality standards are the foundation on which all else is built. Buyers and suppliers are an integral part of any restaurant or foodservice operation. Selecting the optimal buying plan and supplier is paramount. You can select a supplier first and then work together to meet your needs, or you can create specifications for the needed products and request bids from potential suppliers.

Purchasing perishable and nonperishable food products, nonfood products, FF&E, and services requires that purchasers, unit managers, chefs, inventory and receiving clerks, and suppliers and distributors be trained and reliable for their role in the procurement process. Ultimately, you need to be prudent and thorough when determining the operation's buying plan and selecting a supplier who can fully accommodate it.

After completing this chapter, you should be able to:
- Outline the process for procuring products and services.
- Differentiate between perishable and nonperishable food products.
- Understand the importance of assessing and documenting purchasing requirements.
- Define perpetual inventory and physical inventory.
- Identify optimal sources of suppliers.

Chapter 5 Inventory Control

Summary

Calculating product usage, food storage, ordering costs, and estimating product loss is essential to calculating the optimal order size and time. These calculations are integral components of a systematic inventory control system.

While some operations use a perpetual inventory management system, most physically count and value their inventory on a regular basis. Two of the objectives of all operations relative to inventory management are (1) to keep only the needed quantity of food and nonfood products on hand to meet customer needs without experiencing stock-outs, and (2) to *not* maintain more inventory then needed that could result in decreased profits and increased risk due to spoilage, obsolesce, pilferage, or theft.

After completing this chapter, you should be able to:
- Calculate correct order quantities.
- Estimate appropriate timing of orders.
- Explain perpetual and physical inventory systems.

Inventory and Purchasing Practice Questions

Please note the numbers in parentheses following each question. They represent the chapter and page number, respectively, where the content in found in the ManageFirst Competency Guide.

IMPORTANT: These sample questions are designed to familiarize the student with format, length and style of the examination questions, and represent only a sampling of topic coverage.

The grid below represents how the *actual* exam questions will be divided across content areas on the corresponding ManageFirst Program exam.

Inventory and Purchasing	1.	Introduction to Inventory and Purchasing	11
	2.	The Purchasing Function	11
	3.	Quality Standards in Purchasing	14
	4.	The Procurement Process and Supplier Selection	17
	5.	Inventory Control	17
		Total No. of Questions	**70**

The performance level on sample questions does not guarantee passing of a ManageFirst Program examination. Further, the distribution of sample exam questions with their focus on particular areas of subject matter within a ManageFirst Competency Guide is not necessarily reflective of how the questions will be distributed across subject matter on the actual correlating ManageFirst exam.

1. What is the purpose of conducting a goods and services needs assessment? (4, 53)
   A. To provide information to aid in the selection of a vendor
   B. To determine an operation's purchasing requirements
   C. To make the purchaser's job more difficult
   D. To define ordering and receiving procedures

2. How can a foodservice operation maintain a quality standard of purchasing? (1, 5)
   A. Follow an established quality standard for each item or service when purchasing
   B. Forecast future costs of items purchased
   C. Obtain the lowest possible EP or AS price
   D. Analyze outside influences that might affect an operation

3. What is the process by which products and services are chosen based upon quality and cost? (1, 3)
   A. Cooperative buying
   B. Product selection
   C. Maintaining adequate supply
   D. Minimizing investment

4. There are two types of inventory management. What type of system keeps a record or theoretical count of the products placed into and taken from inventory and is continuously updated? (5, 84)
   A. In-process inventory system
   B. Perpetual inventory management system
   C. Physical inventory management system
   D. Management information system

5. What can shopping around for vendors who offer the best prices for goods and services do? (1, 6)
   A. Ensure quality standards are met
   B. Maintain an adequate supply of product
   C. Maintain a foodservice operation's competitive advantage
   D. Anticipate cash needs for a given period

6. What would the Furniture, Fixtures, and Equipment category include? (1, 9)
   A. Computers, insurance, and cash registers
   B. Silverware, candles, and flowers
   C. Utensils, linens, and uniforms
   D. Tables, chairs, and barstools

7. What type of a discount is given if an operation purchases a specified, large amount of a particular product? (2, 23)
   A. Volume discount
   B. Blanket order discount
   C. Promotional discount
   D. Quantity discount

8. What is another term for shrinkage, or product loss as a result of theft? (4, 61)
   A. Spoilage
   B. Pilferage
   C. Receiving
   D. Procurement

9. Why are knowing vendor delivery schedules and the availability of items helpful? (1, 4)
   A. It can maintain a quality standard.
   B. It minimizes investment.
   C. It helps maintain adequate supply.
   D. It can help obtain the lowest possible EP price.

10. What role should the intended use of a product play? (3, 34)
    A. It should be he first thing taken into account when determining product specifications.
    B. It is less important than the packaging of a product when determining quality standards.
    C. It is determined by the size and trim of the product.
    D. It is often overlooked when writing product specifications.

11. What is an example of a technical purchasing skill? (2, 18)
    A. Forecasting sales
    B. Training receiving staff
    C. Preparing bid sheets
    D. Budgeting expenditures

12. What do interpersonal skills include? (2, 19)
    A. Work experience
    B. Organizing the purchasing function
    C. Budgeting expenditures
    D. Cooperating with other managers

13. What can hourly employees help a purchaser determine? (2, 16)
    A. The impact purchasing has on the overall budget of an operation
    B. The tools and products hourly employees need to do their jobs
    C. What type of advertising will work best for the operation
    D. If and when an alteration to the menu is required

14. Forecasting sales is what type of skill? (2, 18)
    A. Conceptual
    B. Technical
    C. Ethical
    D. Interpersonal

15. What method requires that the purchaser determine the level of inventory that must continually be in stock from one delivery date to the next? (5, 76)
    A. Levinson
    B. Product usage
    C. Par stock
    D. Perpetual inventory

16. What best describes how a product is meant to be used, developed, or consumed? (3, 34)
    A. Seasonal availability
    B. Quality standard
    C. Brand name
    D. Intended use

18 Inventory and Purchasing

17. Who should be responsible for writing product specifications? (4, 54)
    A. The purchaser alone
    B. The supplier and the purchaser
    C. The owner and purchaser
    D. The purchaser and the managers

18. If the unit of measure is 1 pound and the amount of cheese needed for one serving is 2 ounces, what is the portion factor? (5, 78)
    A. 2
    B. 4
    C. 6
    D. 8

19. What should a purchaser do to help ensure that the correct item is received? (3, 35)
    A. Change the product specifications
    B. Take the vendor out to dinner
    C. Specify the exact name of an item
    D. Give a price limit to the vendor

20. What determines optimal inventory amount? (5, 74)
    A. The number of suppliers available
    B. Product usage, inventory costs, and food costs
    C. The popularity index of a particular item
    D. The Levinson Method.

21. What is one example of a purchaser's job duties? (2, 20)
    A. Negotiating contracts
    B. Accepting kickbacks
    C. Serving customers
    D. Creating recipes

22. How is inventory turnover defined? (5, 73)
    A. Time it takes for a supplier to replace inventory
    B. Product loss as a result of theft or pilferage
    C. Product loss as a result of spoilage
    D. Time it takes for inventory to move from receiving to consumption

23. What can adequate storage facilities and space help reduce? (4, 61)
    A. Pilferage
    B. Skimming
    C. Spoilage
    D. Inventory

24. What influences the choice of packaging the most? (3, 36)
    A. Intended use
    B. Shelf life
    C. Weight range
    D. Edible yield

25. What are used by receiving personnel to verify that the costs on the purchase order are the prices charged on the invoice? (4, 60)
    A. Rule measures
    B. Calculators
    C. Scales
    D. Temperature probes

26. What service category includes painting, plumbing, and cleaning services? (1, 9)
    A. Maintenance services
    B. Utilities
    C. Support services
    D. Business supplies and services

27. What is the term that describes how an item is processed or preserved prior to being packaged? (3, 39)
    A. USDA grade
    B. Acceptable trim
    C. Product count
    D. Market form

28. What best outlines an operation's product selection and ordering, receiving, storing, and issuing procedures? (4, 53)
    A. Needs assessment
    B. Quality standards
    C. Procurement process
    D. Supplier criteria

29. Consistency, cost effectiveness, and space savings are advantages of what action? (3, 46)
    A. Pouring beverages before busy shifts
    B. Buying seasonally available produce
    C. Purchasing value-added products
    D. Following consumer trends

30. Who is typically charged with monitoring the overall budget of an operation? (2, 16)
    A. General manager
    B. Hourly employees
    C. Marketing department
    D. Sales team

31. What is a benefit of making food from scratch? (3, 47)
    A. Allows a chef to offer a signature dish
    B. Is always preferable to purchasing value-added products
    C. Saves time and space
    D. Offers a consistent level of quality

32. In an independent, single-unit operation to whom would the chef normally report? (2, 15)
    A. Dining room manager
    B. Purchasing director
    C. Owner/general manager
    D. Bar manager

33. What may operations that serve products that require extensive preparation also require? (3, 43)
    A. Vendor training of employees
    B. A higher paid general manager
    C. Unskilled employees that can be trained
    D. Employees with higher skill levels

34. What is an example of a perishable item? (4, 62)
    A. Dry milk
    B. Oil
    C. Cocoa
    D. Beverage alcohols

35. Why do foodservice purchasers compete against one another for the best prices for goods and services? (1, 6)
   A. To maintain a competitive advantage
   B. To determine what to buy
   C. To forecast the number of covers in a given period
   D. To maintain quality standards

36. What is a product that has a long shelf life? (4, 63)
   A. Perishable
   B. Value-added
   C. Nonperishable
   D. Equipment

37. What happens in an operation that uses a physical inventory system? (5, 85)
   A. It only counts in-process inventory.
   B. The operation performs an actual count on a regular basis.
   C. It requires a management information system.
   D. The operation makes theoretical counts on a predetermined basis.

38. A food service operation may have many managers such as the kitchen manager and bar manager. Why must a purchaser talk and work with these managers? (4, 54)
   A. To evaluate an operation's needs
   B. To create an approved supplier list
   C. To develop a replacement and return policy
   D. To define and create sanitation practices

39. Historical usage data is used as a starting point when calculating what? (5, 74)
   A. Expected usage
   B. Portion factor
   C. Edible yield percentage
   D. Order size

40. What organizational structure might a chain operation have?
    (2, 15)
    A. Equipment buyer reports to the commissary
    B. Beverage buyer report to the food buyer
    C. Food buyer report to the purchasing director
    D. Purchasing director report to centralized distribution

Inventory and Purchasing
Answer Key to Practice Questions

1. B
2. A
3. B
4. B
5. C
6. D
7. D
8. B
9. C
10. A
11. C
12. D
13. B
14. A
15. C
16. D
17. D
18. D
19. C
20. B

21. A
22. D
23. C
24. A
25. B
26. A
27. D
28. C
29. C
30. A
31. A
32. C
33. D
34. D
35. A
36. C
37. B
38. A
39. A
40. C

Inventory and Purchasing Explanations to the Answers for the Practice Questions

Question #1
Answer A is wrong. A goods and services assessment assesses an operation's needs and wants. Choosing a vendor requires a set of selection criteria.
Answer B is correct. A common first step in the procurement process is to conduct a goods and services needs assessment to determine an operation's purchasing requirements.
Answer C is wrong. The goods and services needs assessment may be conducted by the purchaser. It is not intended to make the procurement task more difficult.
Answer D is wrong. Ordering and receiving procedures are defined after the goods and services needs assessment has been completed.

Question #2
Answer A is correct. Maintaining quality standards can be more easily achieved by following the operation's established quality standards for each item or service when purchasing.
Answer B is wrong. Forecasting future costs of an item helps minimize investment, not maintain quality standards.
Answer C is wrong. Low EP and AP prices is a purchasing objective that helps maintain competitive advantage.
Answer D is wrong. A purchaser analyzes outside influences that might affect an operation's sales to help maintain an adequate supply of product.

Question #3
Answer A is wrong. Cooperative buying is when independent operations combine orders to buy collectively in order to obtain lower prices.
Answer B is correct. The process by which products and services are chosen based on quality and cost is known as product selection.
Answer C is wrong. An adequate supply of product is maintained to ensure the product is available for sale.
Answer D is wrong. A purchaser must minimize investment because an operation's funds are limited.

Question # 4
Answer A is wrong. In-process inventory keeps track of actual value and actual count of all current inventory.
Answer B is correct. The perpetual inventory system keeps a perpetually updated, theoretical count or record of the products placed into and taken from inventory.
Answer C is wrong. The physical inventory system keeps track of actual value and actual count of all current inventory.
Answer D is wrong. Many foodservice operators believe they must have a management information system to use a perpetual inventory system. The management information system itself is not an inventory system.

Question #5
Answer A is wrong. An operation's quality standards are maintained by following established quality standards for each item or service when purchasing.
Answer B is wrong. An adequate supply of product is maintained to ensure the product is available for sale.
Answer C is correct. Maintaining a competitive advantage can be difficult because competitors rarely disclose their costs and vendors may apply pricing unevenly among establishments; therefore, a purchaser must shop around for the best prices and services available.
Answer D is wrong. Anticipating cash needs helps minimize investment.

Question #6
Answer A is wrong. Computers, insurance, and cash registers are in the business supplies and services category.
Answer B is wrong. Silverware, candles, and flowers are in the nonfood items category.
Answer C is wrong. Utensils, linen, and uniforms are in the nonfood items category.
Answer D is correct. Tables, chairs, and barstools are in the furniture, fixtures, and equipment category.

Question # 7
Answer A is wrong. A volume discount is based on the total amount of product purchased and you may purchase more than a single product to qualify.
Answer B is wrong. A blanket order discount is the same as a volume discount.
See Answer A.
Answer C is wrong. A promotional discount is a reduction on a specific product for
a limited time.
Answer D is correct. A quantity discount is applied when a specified, large amount of a particular product is purchased.

Question #8
Answer A is wrong. Spoilage is when a product is ruined and no longer usable.
Answer B is correct. Both shrinkage and pilferage are terms used to refer to product loss due to theft.
Answer C is wrong. Receiving is the process of checking and either accepting or refusing deliveries.
Answer D is wrong. Procurement is the entire process of ordering, receiving, storing, and issuing product.

Question #9
Answer A is wrong. An operation's quality standards are maintained by following established quality standards for each item or service when purchasing.
Answer B is wrong. One objective of a purchaser is to minimize investment by considering customer count forecasts and anticipated cash needs.
Answer C is correct. A number of tools are used to maintain adequate supply of product including availability of items from vendors and vendor delivery schedules.
Answer D is wrong. Obtaining the lowest possible EP price is another objective of purchasing.

Question #10
Answer A is correct. Quality standards are set according to intended use and further detailed to create product specifications; therefore, intended use is the first thing that must be taken into account when writing product specifications.
Answer B is wrong. The intended use is more important than the packaging.
Answer C is wrong. Size and trim are determined by intended use of a product.
Answer D is wrong. The intended use of an item is never overlooked when writing product specifications.

Question #11
Answer A is wrong. Forecasting sales is a conceptual skill.
Answer B is wrong. Training receiving staff is an interpersonal skill.
Answer C is correct. Preparing bid sheets is an example of a technical skill.
Answer D is wrong. Budgeting expenditures is an example of a conceptual skill.

Question #12
Answer A is wrong. Previous work experience is a desirable quality, but not a skill.
Answer B is wrong. Organizing the purchasing function is a conceptual skill.
Answer C is wrong. Budgeting expenditures is a conceptual skill.
Answer D is correct. Cooperating with other managers is an interpersonal skill.

Question #13
Answer A is wrong. The general manager monitors the overall budget.
Answer B is correct. A purchaser must ensure that hourly workers have the tools and products necessary to do their jobs.
Answer C is wrong. The marketing department is responsible for advertising.
Answer D is wrong. Sales, marketing, or other creative teams might need to be consulted about menu alterations.

Question # 14
Answer A is Correct. Forecasting sales is an example of a conceptual skill.
Answer B is wrong. Forecasting sales is not a technical skill.
Answer C is wrong. Forecasting sales is not an ethical skill.
Answer D is wrong. Forecasting sales is not an interpersonal skill.

Question #15
Answer A is wrong. The Levinson method forecasts the amount of product to order based on each item's consumed portions size relative to that item's sales volume for a specific period. It includes using the par stock inventory level.
Answer B is wrong. Product usage is not a method to calculate optimal inventory amounts.
Answer C is correct. The par stock approach is defined as a method that requires the purchaser to determine the level of inventory that must be continually in stock from one delivery date to the next.
Answer D is wrong. Perpetual inventory does not calculate product usage.

Question #16
Answer A is wrong. Seasonal availability describes products that are not available all year.
Answer B is wrong. Quality standards identify and communicate required product characteristics and specifications to staff and suppliers.
Answer C is wrong. A brand name may imply quality and be requested by a supplier.
Answer D is correct. A product's intended use describes how it is meant to be used, developed, or consumed.

Question #17
Answer A is wrong. The purchaser must work with other managers to assess an operation's needs and write the product specifications.
Answer B is wrong. The supplier is not involved in writing product specifications.
Answer C is wrong. The owner may be involved in developing product specifications, but the responsibility for writing the specifications falls upon the managers and purchaser.
Answer D is correct. It is imperative that a purchaser go back to the managers, after the needs assessment, and together write the product specifications.

Question #18
Answer A is wrong. The student used the wrong formula or inserted data incorrectly.
Answer B is wrong. The student used the wrong formula or inserted data incorrectly.
Answer C is wrong. The student used the wrong formula or inserted data incorrectly.
Answer D is correct. First, one pound must be converted to 16 ounces. The portion factor equation then reads 16 oz. ÷ 2 oz. = 8 oz.

Question #19
Answer A is wrong. Product specifications should be written so that suppliers understand the exact item that is to be supplied.
Answer B is wrong. A vendor should not have to be rewarded or bribed into providing correct items.
Answer C is correct. Exact names should be given in the product specifications to ensure that the correct item is delivered by the supplier.
Answer D is wrong. Price limits do not specify items.

Question #20
Answer A is wrong. The number of suppliers available has no bearing on optimal inventory amount.
Answer B is correct. Knowing product usage, inventory costs, and food costs will help determine the optimal inventory amount.
Answer C is wrong. The popularity index is used in forecasting supply of an item.
Answer D is wrong. The Levinson method is the first step used in calculating product usage.

Question #21
Answer A is correct. A purchaser's job duties include negotiating contracts.
Answer B is wrong. Accepting kickbacks is a serious ethical transgression.
Answer C is wrong. Serving customers is the job of the wait staff.
Answer D is wrong. Creating recipes would be the job of the chef or creative team.

Question #22
Answer A is wrong. A supplier's delivery schedule determines the time it takes for inventory to be replaced.
Answer B is wrong. Shrinkage is the term for product loss due to theft or pilferage.
Answer C is wrong. Spoilage occurs when a product becomes ruined and is unusable.
Answer D is correct. Inventory turnover is the time it takes for the inventory to move from the operation's receiving docks to the table to be consumed by customers.

Question #23
Answer A is wrong. Increased security can reduce pilferage.
Answer B is wrong. Increased security can reduce skimming, also known as pilferage.
Answer C is correct. Product loss due to spoilage can be reduced by having adequate storage facilities and space.
Answer D is wrong. Inventory is protected, not reduced, by adequate storage facilities.

Question #24
Answer A is correct. The intended use of a product is first taken into consideration when choosing a product's packaging type.
Answer B is wrong. A product's shelf life is the amount of time a product can remain suitable for use.
Answer C is wrong. Weight range is part of a product's specifications.
Answer D is wrong. Edible yield is the percent of a product that is usable.

Question #25
Answer A is wrong. Rule measures are used for sampling and confirmation purposes.
Answer B is correct. Calculators are used to verify the costs on the purchase order are the prices charged on the invoice.
Answer C is wrong. Scales are used for sampling and confirmation purposes.
Answer D is wrong. Temperature probes are used for sampling and confirmation purposes.

Question #26
Answer A is correct. Maintenance services include painting, plumbing, and cleaning.
Answer B is wrong. Utilities do not include painting, plumbing, and cleaning.
Answer C is wrong. Support services do not include painting, plumbing, and cleaning.
Answer D is wrong. Business supplies and services do not include painting, plumbing, and cleaning.

Question #27
Answer A is wrong. USDA Grade is a quality measurement provided by the government.
Answer B is wrong. Acceptable trim measures the maximum amount of waste acceptable in a product upon receipt.
Answer C is wrong. Product count is a measurement of the number of items within a certain portion or size.
Answer D is correct. Market form is defined as how an item is processed prior to being packaged.

Question #28
Answer A is wrong. A goods and needs assessment determines an operation's purchasing requirements.
Answer B is wrong. Quality standards identify and communicate required product characteristics and specifications to staff and suppliers.
Answer C is correct. The procurement process outlines an operation's product selection; the ordering, receiving, and storing process; and the issuing policies and procedures.
Answer D is wrong. Supplier criteria are used to select an appropriate supplier.

Question #29
Answer A is wrong. These are the advantages of purchasing value-added products and have nothing to do with pouring beverages in advance of busy periods.
Answer B is wrong. Seasonally available produce may be more expensive and not consistent in its availability.
Answer C is correct. Some advantages of purchasing value-added products are consistency, cost effectiveness, time effectiveness, and space savings.
Answer D is wrong. Consistency, cost effectiveness, and space savings are not related to consumer trends.

Question #30
Answer A is correct. The general manager typically monitors the overall budget and will carefully watch purchasing's spending and performance.
Answer B is wrong. Hourly employees do not monitor the overall budget.
Answer C is wrong. Marketing does not monitor the overall budget.
Answer D is wrong. Sales does not monitor the overall budget.

Question #31
Answer A is correct. One advantage of making food from scratch is the ability to create signature dishes.
Answer B is wrong. This is not always true. A make-or-buy analysis can help determine what should be made internally and what should be bought ready-made.
Answer C is wrong. Buying value-added products, rather than making food from scratch, saves time and space.
Answer D is wrong. Value-added products offer consistency.

Question #32
Answer A is wrong. The chef would not normally report to the dining room manager.
Answer B is wrong. The chef would not normally report to the purchasing director.
Answer C is correct. In a small, independent operation the chef would normally report to the owner/general manager.
Answer D is wrong. The chef would not normally report to the bar manager.

Question #33
Answer A is wrong. A vendor does not normally train employees.
Answer B is wrong. The general manager does not prepare the products.
Answer C is wrong. Products that require extensive preparation also require skilled employees.
Answer D is correct. Products that require extensive preparation also require more skilled employees.

Question #34
Answer A is wrong. Dry milk is a nonperishable item.
Answer B is wrong. Oil is a nonperishable item.
Answer C is wrong. Cocoa is a nonperishable item.
Answer D is correct. Beverage alcohols are perishable items.

Question #35
Answer A is correct. In order to maintain a competitive advantage, food service purchasers must compete against each other for the best prices.
Answer B is wrong. What to buy is determined by the needs of the operation.
Answer C is wrong. Forecasting covers helps an operation maintain an adequate supply of product.
Answer D is wrong. Quality standards are maintained by adhering to an operation's established quality standards for each product and service; and communicating these standards to the vendor.

Question #36
Answer A is wrong. Perishable products have a limited shelf life.
Answer B is wrong. Value-added products are proportioned and processed food items.
Answer C is correct. Nonperishable items have a longer shelf life.
Answer D is wrong. Equipment does not fall under the categories perishable or nonperishable. It is not considered to have a shelf life.

Question #37
Answer A is wrong. A physical inventory requires counting all inventory not just in-process inventory.
Answer B is correct. Physical inventory management requires actual valuing and actual accounting of all inventory on a regular, predetermined basis.
Answer C is wrong. A management information system is thought by many to be required when using a perpetual inventory system.
Answer D is wrong. A perpetual inventory system makes theoretical counts.

Question #38
Answer A is correct. The purchaser must talk and work directly with managers who use the purchased items to decide on both immediate and future needs, in other words to evaluate an operation's requirements.
Answer B is wrong. An approved supplier list is created by the organization, not the purchaser.
Answer C is wrong. The purchaser works with the vendor to develop a replacement and return policy.
Answer D is wrong. States and local municipalities regulate sanitation practices.

Question #39
Answer A is correct. To properly calculate expected usage, you will use historical usage data as a starting point.
Answer B is wrong. The portion factor is calculated dividing the unit of measurement by the amount of an ingredient needed for one serving.
Answer C is wrong. The edible yield percentage is the amount of product that is usable.
Answer D is wrong. The order size is computed by dividing an item's usage by an ingredients portion divider.

Question #40
Answer A is wrong. The equipment buyer reports to the purchasing director.
Answer B is wrong. The beverage buyer reports to the purchasing director.
Answer C is correct. The food buyer reports to the purchasing director.
Answer D is wrong. Centralized distribution reports to the purchasing director.

Inventory and Purchasing Glossary

Acceptable trim   amount of tolerable waste acceptable in a product upon receipt

Approved supplier list   list of suppliers that meet the operation's standards for ethics, reliability, and financial stability

As purchased (AP) price   cost of an item before all trimming, fabrication, and cooking

As served (AS) price   cost of an item as it is served to the customer

Beverage alcohols   drinkable products that contain a significant percentage of alcohol. Examples include beers, wines, and spirits.

Bid buying plan   system that allows for various suppliers to respond to a request-for-bid or request-for-price (RFP)

Bin card   record of when an item was delivered, when it was issued, and, if applicable, when it was returned to storage

Blanket order discount   same as volume discount; a price reduction awarded based upon the total amount of product purchased

Buyer's authority   limits of power the purchaser (buyer) has to accomplish assigned duties

Buyer's responsibility   set of activities managed by the purchaser (buyer)

Capital cost   amount of an operation's money that is used to maintain inventory levels. Also known as *opportunity costs*.

Capital expenditures   FF&E and other items that are expected to last for more than one year

Carrying cost   expense incurred for insuring and maintaining storage space, as well as the costs of spoiled, outdated, or expired items. Also known as *storage costs*.

Cash discount   discount offered in exchange for payment at the time of delivery or according to some other pre-arranged schedule

Cash position   amount of cash available to an operation at a specific point in time

Competitive advantage   favorable relationship or position relative to one or more characteristics of a competitor

Consumer trends   general directions in which a market or consumer behavior is headed

Cooperative or co-op buying   process of joining with others to collectively purchase products

Cost-plus purchasing   arrangement between a buyer and a seller in which the supplier sells their products at cost, plus an agreed-upon supplier markup

Count   measurement of the number of items or units within a certain portion or size

Covers   number of customers served; one customer = one cover

Customer count forecast   estimate of the number of guests to be served in an upcoming accounting period

Customer count history   number of customers and times at which an operation has served those customers in the past

Distributor sales representative   supplier's salesperson

Economic order quantity (EOQ) amount to order which will yield the lowest possible order costs

Economies of scale savings that a multi-unit business generates for itself by sharing the cost of purchasing goods and services

Edible portion (EP) cost cost of a single portion as delivered to the guest

Edible portion (EP) price cost of an item after all trimming and fabrication (but before cooking)

Edible yield amount of usable product acceptable in a purchased item

EP per product unit as purchased (AP) price of an item divided by its edible yield percentage

EP per serving as purchased (AP) price of an item divided by its portion divider (PD)

Forecasted usage/supply of a particular item for this period amount of an item that is anticipated to be used in a defined time period

Franchise business system that an independent owner buys from a company, along with the right to use the company's name, logo, and products

Free sample small amount of goods or equipment offered to an operation at no charge

Furniture, fixtures and equipment (FF&E) capital expenditure items used in a foodservice operation

Goods and services needs assessment review of the (products and services) the operation currently has versus what it ideally needs

Historical usage data   previously recorded customer counts, menu item popularity indices, and analysis of outside influences that should be considered prior to establishing optimal future inventory levels

Individually quick-frozen (IQF)   process in which food is flash frozen in individual pieces prior to packaging

In-process inventory   amount of inventory currently being used in production

Intended use   How a product or service is meant to be used, developed, or consumed

Inventory turnover   amount of time it takes for inventory to move from the operation's receiving area to the guest's table for consumption

Job description   document that describes the specific duties an employee must perform

Job specification   list of the desired knowledge, skills, and abilities a person should possess to successfully perform the functions of a specific job

"Just in time" (JIT) inventory management   purchasing method designed to minimize the amount of product held in inventory between delivery dates

Kickback   money or other gift received by an individual in return for purchasing from a specific vendor

Levinson method   order system that bases the size of the order on historical data and forecasted customer counts

Make-or-buy analysis   assessment that reveals whether a product should be prepared from scratch or purchased in a partially or fully processed market form

Management information system (MIS)   computer aided data gathering and analysis tools designed to assist managers in effectively completing their tasks

Market Form   manner in which an item is processed prior to being packaged

Menu price   selling price of an item. Computation of menu price may vary based upon the pricing system utilized in a specific operation.

Nonperishable products   items that do not support the growth of bacteria that cause spoilage

One-stop shop buying plan   arrangement where the operation selects one (or two) suppliers to meet all of the operation's buying needs

Opportunity cost   amount of an operation's money that is used to maintain inventory levels. Also known as *capital costs*.

Optimal price   lowest possible edible portion cost of an item plus the value added by the product's quality and associated supplier services. Note: the term *optional price* on page 82 should be *optimal price*.

Order size   amount to order that is based upon the number of forecasted portions needed divided by the ingredient's portion divider

Packer's brand name   supplier's own name brand (labeled) product

Par   fully stocked, predetermined inventory level

Par stock approach   system for determining the optimal amount of an item that should be in stock from one delivery date to the next

Percentage of sales volume   inventory valuation method that relates recommended inventory levels to an operation's annual sales volume.

Perishable products   items that are sold or distributed in a form that will experience significant quality deterioration within a limited period of time as a result of the action of bacteria, light, and/or air

Perpetual inventory   record or theoretical count of the products placed into and taken from inventory that is continually (perpetually) updated at a central storage facility

Perpetual inventory management   recording and managing inventory based upon theoretical counts

Perpetual inventory system   process that utilizes a record or theoretical count of the products placed into and taken from inventory and that is continually (perpetually) updated

Physical inventory   real (physical) count of inventory items and their value

Physical inventory management   process of managing inventory that relies upon a real (physical) count of inventory items

Pilferage   theft of small amounts of inventory. Also called *inventory skimming* or *shrinkage*. Often committed by employees of an operation.

Plan of action (POA)   series of procurement steps that take into account the products that best meet the operation's wants and needs and the suppliers that can best provide them according to the operation's documented quality standards and buying practices

Popularity index   measure of the popularity of a specific menu item in relation to other items in its category and the popularity of one menu category relative to other categories

Portion controlled (PC)   proportioned, individually wrapped single servings

Portion divider (PD)   number of portions available in one portion (or other appropriate measure) after the item's edible yield is considered

Portion factor (PF)   number of portions available in one pound (or other appropriate measure)

Procurement   entire process by which products and services are selected

Procurement process   operation's product selection, ordering, receiving, and storing processes, as well as the issuing of policies and procedures related to achieving the operation's procurement mission and goals

Product selection   process by which products and services are chosen based upon quality and cost

Product specification   written characteristics of a particular product

Profit   money remaining after all operating expenses have been paid

Promotional discount   price reductions offered on selected products or for specially designated periods of time

Purchase order   when submitted via paper, a multi-part form that stipulates what product or service is wanted and when it is wanted; when submitted via computer, a saved purchase order file

Purchase requisition   internal procurement document that details, to a buyer, a department's product needs before an order is placed

Purchasing   obtaining products of a desired quality at a desired price

Purchasing skill set   group of skills and competencies buyers need to successfully complete their assigned tasks

Quality standards   required product standards and specifications

Quantity discount   price reduction resulting from the purchase of a large amount of a particular product

Ready-to-go   items issued to the production unit in the form in which they will be consumed

Receiving   process of checking and then either accepting or refusing deliveries

Reciprocity   arrangement in which a buyer agrees to buy from a vendor in return for some kind of return business from that vendor

Reorder point   number of units to which on-hand inventory must be reduced before an additional order should be placed

Request-for-bid   invitation, issued by a buyer to a vendor, to provide a bid for supplying a requested item

Request-for-price (RFP)   invitation, issued by a buyer to a supplier, to provide a firm price for supplying a requested item

Route salespeople   vendor delivery staff who repeatedly deliver, assess inventory, and then stock an operation's supply of goods to bring them up to par level

Shelf life   amount of time during which a product can remain suitable for use

Spoilage   condition that exists when a product's quality has diminished to the point that it is no longer meets the operation's quality standard and is unusable

Standard cost   same as *standard serving cost* but for a single item

Standard serving cost   sum of the individual edible portion (EP) costs for items making up a combination plate

Steward sales   another term for personal sales; purchases by employees to take advantage of the company's purchasing power

Stockless purchasing   method of buying that permits an operator to purchase a large quantity of a product at the current price, but directs the supplier to store it and deliver it to the operation as it is needed

Stockout   term used to describe a situation when an item has been depleted from inventory

Storage area regulations   rules that detail who can enter and remove items from the storage areas. Storage area regulations should be strictly enforced.

Storage cost   expense incurred for insuring and maintaining storage space, as well as the costs of spoiled, outdated, or expired items. Also known as *carrying costs*.

Throughput   measure of the speed at which service requests are processed

Total annual costs   amount of money required per year to order and store a menu item

Value-added products   term used to describe proportioned or processed items

Vendor   company that sells a product or service

Volume discount   price reduction awarded based upon the total amount of product purchased